And the eyes are brilliant is your army!

Threads, spinning wheels, the rock of fate!

Iliyan Yurukov

PARTRIDGE

To order additional copies of this book, contact
Toll Free 800 101 2657 (Singapore)
Toll Free 1 800 81 7340 (Malaysia)
orders.singapore@partridgepublishing.com

www.partridgepublishing.com/singapore

CONTENTS

And the eyes are brilliant is your army! 1

Spain! 5

Between Egypt, Mesopotamia, and the Hittites! "To
    understand the present, you must understand
    the past!" Confucius! 7

Old men! 11

Legal protection of children! First lady! 13

Football in England! 15

"I am the One!" Waiting! 17

Sabayon spoon! Determinism! 21

Treaty, Golan Heights! 23

Secrets of life! 25

Purim and modernity! 29

The first day of the Mayan calendar!
    Date of death of Atlantis! 31

Sahara, a herd of cattle near the village! 35

ECG! 39

Solomon! 41

In the country of St. Valentine! 45

You are a producer queen! 49

Holocaust! 51

Stem cells! 53

Tu B'Shvat! 55

120 beginning of life, the mystery of the queen! 57

Adam! 61

Catherine, Williams! 63

Queen, surrealism, and photography!..65

Business Portal!..67

Christmas tree in Jerusalem!...71

Salvation Army!..75

"About the dignity of man!" (Giovanni Picot della Mirandola)!........79

Ah girls fashionistas, in Prado and look! 83

Holiday lights, Maccabee! 87

The secret of the name of Shakespeare! (Edouard de Ver.)! 91

Adele Bloch-Bower!..95

Thread spinning, fate!..97

Israel! 99

AND THE EYES ARE BRILLIANT
IS YOUR ARMY!

Look at the table wine.
Birthday is it!
In the glasses is in store, it is royal.
Is there an excerpt ?, Wow!
And the tea is not a sin.
Let all support you!
Here is a bunch of enzymes, what?
Honor nature, life and all.
Cell please be good.
So always, always young.
Virtue, positive.
He will always add strength.
Honor the prayer and the weather.
And the story is so much.
And customs rest.
Wisdom is important, that with you!
In years of very difficult, you always dare.
How we love England!
Copper she gave and Arthur fate.
And we love to design, sometimes watch.
London is beautiful, there is something to warm.
Eternal queen, you are Elizabeth.
As you noticed us, please us.
Birthday, also God's path.
How much did the mighty country teach us?
Ah, Oxford friendly, Jerusalem couple...

After all, the east piggy bank, wisdom in full.
You fought with the infection, escaped from the fire.
The queen is clever, you are friends with science.
You are slim in the navy, strong in economics.
How did Dumas love you? Glorified not in vain.
Look how lovely all your sons are.
Burbach though small, but you lit.
And the eyes of the soldier is your army!
Gallery!

SPAIN!

Flamenco you are graceful.
How much beauty.
Colors are kaleidoscopic.
Try, catch up.
How many, many, charm.
Symmetry link.
Is there anything neutral?
Yes that you, everything is uniform.
Leticia, flowers.
Gallery!

Between Egypt, Mesopotamia, and the Hittites! "To understand the present, you must understand the past!" Confucius!

The sun you big power
Changed and stoked.
Destroyed your punishment.
Deprived fate.
Rain cometary.
Bronze century.
Ah volcanoes, man.
Neil Milah, Sahara Chahla, for animals that bad weather.
In the Dead Sea gray splash.
And basalts up and up.
All fire, heat arrow.
What is Gomorrah? Oh my God!
Ah, Sodom you look!
Everything shakes like gases are evil.
Sulfur ball there inside.
Their cities suddenly disappeared.
Fee, cracks, trawls.
Everything asphalt glittered.
Troy emptied, suffered.
Abraham did you go, what is it?
Lot and you survived.
The trace of the sculpture, crystal style.
Disasters, weather style.

Aggravated all adversity.

The planetary-scale here.

And the flood is not just after horror, nightmares.

Will roofing repeat again?

Atlantis is not smog.

Laser scary affairs.

Better peace and humanism.

Ecology prestige.

Collectively, all is good.

Humanity award.

Bibi you stood to the end!

What would Motherland blossom?

The world welcomes you!

Gallery!

OLD MEN!

Old men are sick, you are at home!
It's hard to walk that som!
Who in flight, abroad!
Retirement homes, airport.
But the Motherland is waiting for you.
Do not reach you, hard.
Who will help? Time is waiting.
Gallery!

LEGAL PROTECTION OF CHILDREN! FIRST LADY!

You are persistent, persistent.
And beautiful, like Madonna.
Highly gifted., Raphael is your path.
For children, all your love.
Like design, architecture!
And proportions, Confucius
It is plastic, color, long.
Temperament star.
The tale is given to everyone.
Children as it is needed.
What is fashion is a hit!
The difference gives everyone.
To be always successful.
You need to be gentle to the child.
Give him warmth.
Learning link.
The market means of labor.
Flourishing villages, cities.
Here is the analysis, height.
Peace for you is always friends.
Gallery!

Football in England!

Catherine, Williams, kids.
Kings of football, yes.
Katherine, you are a goalkeeper, a star.
The hobbies are strong.
How many workouts are there?
Everyone is strong, very clever.
The color of the shirt is light.
After all, football, so he flies away.
A race walk! For children, she is kind.
Horseback riding here, for the family she is sweet.
There are favorites and labor!
Of course the helicopter. he is waiting for knowledge of dad.
And pictures, mother's code.
I will play with the baby, hc is very sweet.
And smart, golden.
What will he like? He will find his path, it is difficult forever in sight.
Harry, Megan, great.
In sports, you are the Olympics creators.
Obey the seas.
Sport for you, love, holy.
Gallery!

"I am the One!" Waiting!

You are predicted by Moses.
Pharaoh of my passions.
And Vivaldi praised.
He created the score.
Grew up in a great country.
You studied like everyone else.
Respected you all yard.
But you saved your people.
Pyramids, Sphinxes here.
Unusually all around.
Who built the Pyramids?
Mummy glory, who foresaw?
Ba and Ka! What is Atlantis?
Milestone vibrations of thin lines.
Here the genome was praised.
Who are you in the future? What is in it?
We are still friends with the past.
What is predicted? Not so easy.
Longevity on the go? You are almost parents!
What is the custom? Understand the meaning!
Gene program, complex cartogram.
We must donate blood.
And the computer will read everything.
Should we change the genome? Every gene is a gnome.
If in the future there is a risk?
What to visit statistics?
Michio Kaku leads us, is it promising, what is waiting for?

That children will always help, she will oblige immunity to live.
Can old age be treated? It is unpleasant, we must live!
Israel has successes, genes, years, the gift of nature.
Evolutions turn, all diseases change.
We have immortal fathers.
Abraham and Moses, food of the best examples.
Homeland always love! Look at the tree of life!
Solomon's print, the alphabet of our numbers to become.
There is to be so in the head! Well, of course not in the tail.
If I suddenly do not believe? Am I losing victory?
Gallery!

Sabayon spoon! Determinism!

The mystery was everlasting, with the queen, beauty.

She loved incense, measure knew and talent.

Measuring spoon, hole, marks, numbers, their effects.

The aroma is so tart, sweet and curative, gamma, style.

How graceful are the bushes, and under the sun, the sky grew?

Preserved ridge, curious, so attracted.

How the call of flowers loved gardens and nature.

Solomon visited, the tree of life distinguished.

What beauty appreciated, mind that melts water.

The king is beautiful, very wise.

The queen conquered the rumor.

How much logic and taste?

Analysts have the keys., He can hear everything.

That riddles and comparisons, led to a conversation, a genius.

And the hyperbolas are bright, that analysis, synthesis, you.

Wisdom is a companion of beauty.

What is the reason? Consequences, observations.

And teaching methods.

And a love of custom, kind.

Intuitions of their realities.

Memory, memory is the arrow.

What a hunch how easy?

Who wrote? "Song of Songs"! A dialectic of all kings.

And today is the light, look! Bibi! Trump! Elizabeth!

Gallery!

Treaty, Golan Heights!

Signed a contract, very important to us with you.

Here is the Sacred Land.

People world, it is a symbol, shelter.

Peaceful days of prospects, Trump and Bibi the meaning is as follows.

A region of great heights, historical pillars.

There civilization edge, Eikumeny area.

The path passed here Abraham.

Ancestral and custom call.

Life is sacred and holy.

Where is the beginning? There is no end.

Diplomacy is the world!

A century of discovery, honor fathers.

Here is the migration path.

And they are not easy.

Those by consensus are nice.

God's will fastened.

Gallery!

Secrets of life!

The ocean is a mystery, mystery.
The brain is different and talent.
Who 400 lives?
Phosphorus gently saves.
Single-celled too.
Millions of years come by.
What did nature give them?
Always keeps them.
Everything, everything is connected in the world.
Forest and the brain and the Earthshine.
DNA secrets are many.
The relationship is darkness in nature.
There are stored maps of the world.
Knowledge, what is the genus on the air?
Are we like animals?
Is food good? Will help?
Eykumen than plentiful?
What is there water and reefs?
If mountains and valleys?
Chemistry is important because there are reasons.
Medicine, surgery.
And hormones are avalanche here.
There is a jellyfish orchid.
Secrets that a snake, a picture.
What about regeneration moves?
The brain that gave sunrises?
Amnesia is there a gathering?

Does that pass? The gift of nature.
Here the Japanese say.
Everybody is a hail.
Cell bright then parade?
Would anyone cascade?
What are the particles? Hydra what?
Shared? So what?
Suddenly took recovered.
The tail of the mouse fell off.
Then the Spaniards dismantled.
Cells, cells caressed.
That would restore the brain?
You think what a rhythm?
Naturally the best.
Maybe the currents are light?
What is the regeneration secret?
Maybe this is the secret of the Vedas?
Gallery!

PURIM AND MODERNITY!

Mom see Purim!
I used the crown, you can make up!
To cherries eyes, then my story.
My grandmother Esther, that would go to her to Rome.
Who were you then?
When a schoolgirl, beautiful.
There will be carnival everywhere.
How many epigrams are there?
We have a queen in class.
She sits on the desk on the left.
Homes joy and flowers.
See photos.
Books you gave me.
How was it in history?
Yes! Of course, she is sad.
After all, my people love.
There are rattles and Haman.
After all, the custom is dear to us.
We need peace in a year.
Let Israel bloom spring!
Call to Paris, Canada!
And in America we are welcome.
London, Harry, naughty!
The Louvre is beautiful and dear.
What costumes carnival?
In all countries, happiness is there.
Our Israel is nice!
He reads Torah and friends.
Bibi, he loves children.
Gallery!

THE FIRST DAY OF THE MAYAN CALENDAR!
DATE OF DEATH OF ATLANTIS!

The past world of civilizations, Aquarius the sign of the
coronations!
Disaster movements of chances.
And predictions and struggles.
Wiener Light, but where did you come from?
Mu left and Maya became you all tirelessly.
Settled and worked, secretly taught knowledge.
Kukulkan you are the Deity, that intrigue and a link.
The serpent feathered on pillars, he entered into all the canons.
Yucatan then Mother Earth.
Eternal impulse through the ages.
In the universe, what is the earth?
Galaxy calendar dawn.
Polynesia and Easter Island.
You stories involved.
What is migration? Of the year.
Firstborn, star.
Here is the Egypt Pyramid.
52 degrees then rhythm?
What are the straits, Ocean?
How did you cross them?
Clash, volcanoes.
How did you accurately calculate?
Time is always a mystery.
What is space? Myth? Creativity?

How is the soul protected?
What about the future? Dream?
Does that memory?
Life is always holy!
They will remember to honor the Father!
Moses is known, yes?
All that came true!
What is the future bridge?
Diplomacy outpost.
Gallery!

Sahara, a herd of cattle near the village!

The art of Neolithic, mysterious, elite.

And secrets covered.

Rock carvings, how fiery it is.

Story link.

As if the disaster, was in the blink of an eye.

Churned instinct by chance you help out.

Movement and rhythm, as you are intertwined.

Have any of them been saved?

Comet Do, carriage.

Birth of the Planet.

What is the event here?

Here are other and influx.

The movement of the Earth is not visible even mist.

Nature You are sons!

The key is strong!

They are mysterious,

Who could they be saved?

Caves you stayed?

So that we do not forget, the nature of fear, sadness.

Since then, the relocation.

And the glacier movement.

As a memory instant.

And the poles are questioned.

Here are the megaliths, Stonehenge shadows.

Tribes mixed up.

Well, where is the earth here?
The desert came to life.
The wells are full.
Here the Beer-Sheva system.
Movement rest.
Gallery!

ECG!

ECG tell whose gift?

You are the whole universe flock.

How did you get into the triangle?

What is the heart?

Whose movie are you?

How many secrets in you are burning?

Who asked you a wave?

Transformation, leap.

Fit into the cam.

Calculate your path.

Is the person on your shoulder?

Are we the same?

Pain, signs, look.

That volcano, the explosion is big.

Tired of that with you?

Here is the story of the Planet.

ECG, how are these secrets?

Conan Doyle, is this grille?

Plasma something to us with greetings?

Is it possible for us to know there?

What would you charge again?

Who invented the scripts?

Congratulations you were a smart guy!

Gallery!

Solomon!

Coral polyps, elite builders.

Atolls are your myths.

And right out of the water, they removed the lime.

Their line is slim as she is overgrown.

Under the weight of the layers.

Pressed them to build.

The foundation is golden.

The construction of the islands.

But look at the lagoon.

There are rings and lakes.

The tides here are azure.

Here to draw and think.

Animal community.

Fish plants are trendy here.

The exchange of the substance of nature.

Plants created all this genius.

Here is Quiet and Indian.

Israeli solid.

There are red colors.

How fiery the water is!

Here are shallows of corals.

And the climate is always strange.

Desert lush Hell.

And the miracle cascade.

Indian is a brother.

Bab el-Mandeb matchmaker.

There are no rivers.

The strait is beautiful, the centuries here are a trace.
How narrow were the aisles?
How mysterious are the moves here?
Solomon. he is in the Red Sea.
The owner of all spaces.
Ah, ships in the trade.
Their technology is slim.
Phoenician cedar in the lobe.
Bamboo is plastic in the sea.
What are the Aztecs? What is water?
Gold, how big is its price?
Gallery!

IN THE COUNTRY OF ST. VALENTINE!

Valentine's Day.
How many myths in this Rome.
Putti of tender beauty.
Ah, Valeria, dreams!
What is Spartacus? Trakian military.!
Have you been blue-eyed?
Was the prince? Are you good?
But you will not kill the Roman.
Rome, there is the Vatican.
There was a lot of dramas too.
Amazons and tournaments.
And you won the plague.
Transplantation was known.
The blood was then transfused.
Medical gifts were developed, bold.
What kind of baths and bridges?
Caracalla is that you?
Botticelli sang.
Those Madonna, a wonderful gift.
Rafael excavated knew.
Equinox noted.
Tapestry eternal title.
The Museum of England stores.
And Israel knew love.
Look, Napoleon.
Macedonian Second Temple.
How much wisdom? Love
Well, what if Solomon?

"Song of Songs"! Did he love
Very dark beauty.
I admired the wisdom, yes.
Lod, of course, our handsome.
There lives Scheherezade.
And of course Shakespeare.
He is a Verona citizen.
Rome thanks you all.
Valentine's Day.
And the fountain of Bernini. light colored.
He then greeted the whole world.
Gallery!

YOU ARE A PRODUCER QUEEN!

You are a producer queen!
You're a queen producer
And the scripts are made bold.
Very fashionable entourage, the whole history of the passage.
Diplomacy is fate.
We are waiting for titles.
The path is high.
Gallery!

HOLOCAUST!

Holocaust how many tears?
Pain in the heart gives.
Memory eternity in you will ignite.
We pray ahead.
"Schindler's List", Alice!
We are grateful, glows.
You are wide-hearted
This is a great feat.
"Poison your" Planet Sun
Protecting us is not easy.
Everyone is honored with glory.
Who is dead? He will not die!
The world is the holy stubble.
You keep our housing.
And the departed are not alive.
That cannot be repeated.
Torah, you teach us to keep the world
And give love to children.
If they were alive?
That diseases would be conquered!
Gallery!

Stem cells!

Electron and cell.
Developed aptly.
Mind stirred up.
The shares winked.
Memory deployed.
Days in labor are gone.
Stem cells.
Brain sang, kids.
Didactic games.
Signs, symptoms.
Distinction and similarity.
Memory, excellence.
And diet, is it important?
Torah, you're always a carriage.
Groats and souffles, fish, tea in me.
Cells, cells, naughty.
Is life rejuvenated in me?
Ah the Japanese, you loved the energy.
Gallery!

Tu B'Shvat!

We love our country.
That is beautiful, all in bloom.
We drained the swamps.
After all, color, love of nature.
Here are almonds, acacia bush.
Work hard to revive the flowering spirit.
The settlers you could.
You laid gardens.
The temple was worn in the old days.
Tithing in labor.
Supported those foundations.
Sonarodnik and Torah.
For health and in love.
You keep the custom.
Landscapes are so colorful.
There will be new fruits.
Herzl also planted here.
Inspired by understood.
This is a future gift.
Fortunately, he wished the country.
You not only plant.
With piety, save.
Then build roads.
And beautiful bridges.
My Israel is wonderful you.
Always bloom.
Gallery!

120 BEGINNING OF LIFE, THE MYSTERY OF THE QUEEN!

Color photography, riddles eternal face.

Shades a lot of developed.

Souls, gusts, cry.

Nature is grateful, and life is colorful as a myth.

See the whole world is the whole!

Contradictions of genius.

Here in search of a solution.

Art is also a vigil.

Amazing landscape

Rare subtleties of the passage.

You solved riddles.

What is life? And the code is paint.

A moment of discovery ahead.

Mystery color spectrum you.

Whispered that flowers?

This holiness save!

Does intellect have flowers?

Yes, they are all reasonable.

That prophecy ahead.

Longevity will be days.

Mira inner spirit.

Certainly, he is a prophet.

Installations are so important.

You change the future.

With the universe, we are lucky.

Energetics are close.
Information exchange.
An hour of great change.
We meet with scientists.
The secrets of life to learn.
Power fields here.
What are these anchors?
Earth is part of the universe it is true.
Knowledge of life is strong.
Gallery!

ADAM!

How many evenings?

We sat waiting for Comrade.

We tried our best.

You were the navel of the earth for us.

It was the evening, look at least where?

Represented that theater.

And the tickets are all taken.

If there is no like, then busy, do not be angry!

You are an editor, we are poets.

We waited for this applause.

In the chair, you sit probably.

And we are waiting, you can not hear.

How many topics have we gone through?

How many rhymes have we defended?

And then Israel found out about us.

And the task gave us.

It was hard how to understand.

What is important here what to write?

And Oded helped us.

Grammatical channel.

10 years later, you will write in the evening.

Gallery!

CATHERINE, WILLIAMS!

Catherine, Williams!
Catherine, Williams, what a pair!
You are the beginning, of all beginnings.
The real you punished.
Grandma so everyone at the sight for sore eyes.
Aunt, uncle here is communication.
Harry, Megan, great.
The people of England blossom!
Children, joy, and character.
Training, specialty.
Catherine we all congratulate.
And the tiara sparkles like that.
And Israel is winter here.
And It is cold.
But hot hearts.
Up to 120 always.
Gallery!

Queen, surrealism, and photography!

The mirror reflects the world
Visible to two.
Panorama will float, it can be a whole year.
Lighting, rays, reveals that? Look
What's down? What's up?
Behind you love them.
It radiates memory, gaze.
What about the future? Space!
What is imagination?
Would you look into the measurement?
Maybe we should be young?
There is suddenly asking for it.
What is Earth's slope now?
What is the spectrum? The length of pi?
What is Earth gravity?
What is the time, speed, opinion?
Have another hobby?
To Vog here, eternal aspiration.
What is a paradox?
Stay better, here.
Understand time, measure.
Young people love their opinion.
Gallery!

Business Portal!

God of commerce, that's how!
Ah, mercury will smile to us now.
Technology is the highest class.
What offer for us?
Well, we are not in debt.
Thoughts are all in our run.
If we invent something.
We will offer. How? How much?
Shoot us a flea.
Well, have long been running.
Michelangelo could do anything.
He calculated the flight path.
Here's a treat and compose.
And the reasons to find.
Our Solomon was smart.
And the diamond is great and he.
The information is so crowded.
The world is always so wonderful.
Everything has already been invented.
What can we now?
You see here furs you are a squall.
Princess fun carnival.
Glamorous persons and business.
And firms are known and what!
Here heels, watches, manto.
Of course, everything is great.

Prosperitet everywhere around.

And people are the best in everything.

Yes, there is a bill, a bill.

Portrait of Elizabeth, country.

See here the wedding procession.

And sports painting, set and technology is the best light.

Known Torah and Earth.

And Bibi, diplomacy, for peace, she.

Gallery!

CHRISTMAS TREE IN JERUSALEM!

Take a look, Jerusalem!
He is beautiful and loved.
Our children are very bright, picturesque.
Those are warmly dressed now.
Here is a Christmas tree for them.
Here the garlands are just a myth.
Gold, crackers.
Gentle toys.
King David and the harp.
Stories involved.
Congratulations from all countries.
The world is waiting for the midnight hour.
We have friends around the world.
Santa Claus where are you? Where are you?
Lush Christmas trees outfit.
Friendship! World! So in good time!
Love London, eternal Rome!
And Spain's motive.
How many trees are there in the world?
Let him be happy, Paris, Egypt.
There is a skating rink in America.
Skaters, dance, rock.
In a winter fairy tale, the White House.
Submission is coming.
Tales for kids.
Older can and late.
And we are all waiting for gifts.

Grandmothers and grandfathers.
With you, we are always warmer.
Kensington Palace
So many warm hearts there!
How many grandchildren and love!
Oh gifts, you see!
And in Germanium bazaars.
Everything is thought out in advance.
And in Japan always.
The doll rejoices, yes.
Congratulations to all of you, friends!
Gallery!

SALVATION ARMY!

The army is so sweet.
Intellect and power.
Technology build.
Assistant gold.
With Cosmos is friendly.
Protects one.
Girls husbands.
For the people you are friends.
Who saves us from the tsunami?
From the enemies and sel guards.
Pilots are important beautiful.
And extinguish the fire wonderfully.
If they donate blood.
Those are healthy, they are all honored.
Always protect them.
Diplomats us a star.
Trump, Milanya, and Ivanka.
They, after all, serve even in the civilian world.
Lizabeth and Katherine, Megan.
Our Sara, we will celebrate.
Merkel is also great.
That authority is everywhere.
Managed perfectly.
After all, a warrior is not so decent.
Better then warn.
After all, my heart hurts.
And we still have girls.

Those honors and stoics.
To not bury them.
Youth happiness, live.
Do not offend those who are older.
Up to 120 teams.
And the boar is cute.
Loves ladies, wear a tie, happiness to you.
Gallery!

"ABOUT THE DIGNITY OF MAN!"
(GIOVANNI PICOT DELLA MIRANDOLA)!

Oh, the French were surprised.

The Japanese have no linear perspective.

Asymmetry is fresh.

Panorama, the transition to another, yes.

The connection of the universal is brief.

The sense of perception, depth, impatient.

Transition, weather, light, and a jump, but what about the whole, how is its turn?

The refraction of the spectrum, colors, brightness, a circle is noticeable.

"100 landscapes" that noted?

Here the moon and snow, a very dark forest.

Lake, Wednesday, the sign of motion of eternity, the Earth.

Human subject, Fujia, worship object.

Myths and rites, interests trail.

Man you moment, not immortal, but great.

Will, knowledge, omens.

You are Divine, Cosmos is bright.

What is nature, and what am I?

How to tie you, me?

Point the whole system.

Have you been studied in general?

What is movement? Evolutions aspiration?

And the exchange of energy of opinions.

Information plexus.

What are the wave and direction? The reflection of moments.
A twist, a repetition, there is a leap and a painter vigil
Brush tell whether that storm?
What is a tsunami? Moon building
Do we win with you?
Here is nature, man.
The measure, there is a milestone boundary.
What discoveries? Success.
Security, thirst for all.
Longevity is weight.
Gallery!

Ah girls fashionistas, in Prado and look!

Ah, boar you are like an ancestor.
Or something next to it.
An anthropologist is your thesis.
We will advance into the centuries.
They lived like the Earth.
But with consciousness in mind.
They were angry and harsh.
Labyrinths you gave?
But however, life is ahead.
Homo sapiens you have a code?
"Kalevala," explained.
In the sky, there is something shining.
Of course, the ice was white.
And who were the pilots?
Trump Tsunami Wins.
Waves he outwitted.
What is the motion of the earth? And the glow of the moon?
That the Indians could know.
Cycles, cycles from the universe You came.
Well, we all prayed.
The film watched, convinced.
A man with a head.
He solved the laws.
And now he will collect the Christmas tree from the needle.
It will shine valiantly.
And Malanyu glorifies.

Here are the kids amused.
If Megan comes out here.
Harry gives a hand.
Here Wintour.
And a beautiful fashion tour.
A queen with a mirror is talking about something.
Maybe something eternal smooth it creates?
Youth orders, beauty gives.
The world is always beautiful, you promise success.
Debit, credit converges.
Bank favors.
But a fleet is in order.
Andrew is watching him out.
Merkel is always working.
Yachts are just miracles.
There are family cabins.
How cozy they are.
But Israel and it is blooming.
Yes, as sings.
How many clinics and hospitals?
Bibi our you just hit.
After all, 120 is not a myth.
In the New Year, he will congratulate us
Smile, it will become easier.
Weddings, whole weddings beat.
That the Lord loved the country.
Gallery!

Holiday lights, Maccabee!

Hanukkah! Lights!

Hanukkah, love!

The temple lit up.

8 days prayed.

Lifestream broke.

Put a candle in the center.

Maccabees glory.

They remained.

Fertile Land.

You are rich and strong.

She is very holy to us.

Torah glorious trail.

You are the minor, the tree of life.

You confess thoughts.

Catch impulses from hands.

Our requests are here forever.

Someone in the future will read.

Heroism is the commendable friend.

Imprint, tears, prayers.

Even the years will not erase.

The color of the minor is a symbol of will.

In the universe, the role model.

Here the story itself.

Communication you with God, as good.

Past lives do not return.

Is it possible to forget them?
What is the air captured?
Then all the poets will understand.
How much pain and hope?
After all, the inexplicable property.
Waiting for science miracles.
That and in the future beauty.
You have to explain everything.
Gallery!

THE SECRET OF THE NAME OF SHAKESPEARE! (EDOUARD DE VER.)!

Shakespeare's theater here.

Elizabeth loved.

Literature defended.

Researchers encouraged.

British playwright, writer.

What is the status (Edouard de Vere of the nobility?

Sonnets composed, recognition found.

Art you are a philosopher of consciousness an apostrophe.

The culture of society strengthens.

Habits give, imitation rhythm.

Grinds that and the right.

And democracy glory.

He knew languages perfectly.

Theater brightly inspired.

And your guardian Cecil.

In the relationship, you are known to him.

There are many similarities with the hero.

Here underlined nobility.

You have changed only the name.

Your nickname is happy.

Shakespeare, imagination.

Your release.

Not preserved underscore.

Guessings only for the sketch.

England here economy is mythical.

Literature, fleet, beautiful and personal.

Tradition, prosperity model.

It goes deep into the gray centuries.

Israel is also a parable.

Ah, Solomon, the people are proud of you.

Good taste, you knew the product.

He did not stint goldly.

The world has called him the wisest!

And Trump, the code and the institute.

He will learn everything, find the key.

Elizabeth for England is holy.

Politician, diplomat. and you yourself warrior.

Gallery!

ADELE BLOCH-BOWER!

Klimt Austrian magician decor!
Eroticism and passion of enthusiasm.
Kiss your love.
He is sacred to the soul.
And posters perky, catchy.
Narrate what is in Tosca.
The rhythm of the ornament, figures.
Fractional, bright, bright tour.
"Modern style" and nostalgia!
How much sun do you have mercy on?
Compositions gift of the gods.
I love you to let me.
And landscapes and portraits!
How many sacraments and in this!
There are so many color spots here!
What are the scales and plots?
Even in the movies your idol.
And see all the dreams!
Do not solve the creators.
All the beautiful museum.
Gallery!

Thread spinning, fate!

Thread spinning, fate!
You are displaced in space.
Will you stay there?
Are we at the finish line?
If you suddenly remove the fate?
Can I start all over again?
Will the face of spring be repeated?
Or to the new bridges?
Is it possible to change the world?
Young people mounts.
What will I happen there again?
Or should it last?
The world in the worlds, in the space of holes.
Eros of the Greeks, the world is one.
Mystery, mystery sealed.
Solve it, what am I?
Patch his hole.
In another world, I fall?
Pyramids, drive.
You are an energy giver.
Age, the place will continue?
What is now going to happen?
Until the end of everything to know everything.
I would not be in a hurry again.
Who are you?
Do you know
Elected?
You!
Gallery!

ISRAEL!

Trump will always support us.
Our mountains, forest, water.
They are God's friends. Fish Mozart loves that.
There is also a bald mountain.
She does not bloom for a long time.
Is there a reason for that?
Guess what secret?
What do we have, the Internet?
Facebook is also a color.
For poems, the etiquette.
The whole script is here. Photos, spring.
Fashion is the best of all. Food is tasty and satisfying.
And kosher and light.
Wine bouquet and honey.
Weddings, pleasure awaits you.
What kind of cold? Hardened we are yes.!
What dream is there? To 120 years of relatives!
We are waiting for the movie you "Crown"! England hi Madonna.
Bibi in the jacket look.
Just like us.
Children with facets, beautiful.
In jackets fashionable and warm.
Hot summer, what is winter? Color mittens, suffering.
But, what about summer?
Ais drink, tea, flowers.
Gallery!

Printed in the United States
By Bookmasters